—An Illustrated History —

"The Life of Nichiren Daishonin and the Transmission of the True Law"

EDITOR/SUPERVISOR

NICHIREN SHOSHU HEAD OFFICE

© 2020 DAINICHIREN PUBLISHING CO., LTD
546-1 KAMIJO FUJINOMIYA SHIZUOKA JAPAN 418-0116

Foreword

On this occasion, we are pleased to present *The Life of Nichiren Daishonin and the Transmission and Perpetuation of the True Law*, published by the Dai-Nichiren Publishing Co. Ltd. In 1981, Nichiren Shoshu published *The Life of Nichiren Daishonin* (Nichiren Daishonin Shoden) to commemorate the 700th anniversary of the passing of Nichiren Daishonin. For more than 700 years, the Nichiren Shoshu priesthood and laity have correctly revered the Daishonin's life, uninfluenced by mistaken interpretations or traditions that spread over the ages. In recent years, the Treasure Hall building at the Head Temple Taisekiji has been featuring various exhibits, and beginning in April of 2011, the permanent exhibition of "The Life of Nichiren Daishonin" has been on display. Through viewing numerous artworks and photos, one can learn about the Daishonin's lifetime instruction, based on the spirit of *rissho ankoku* (securing the peace of the land through the propagation of true Buddhism); *haja-kensho* (refuting heretical or erroneous views and elucidating correct views and the true teaching); and *shishin guho* (never begrudging one's life for the sake of propagating the Law). These are fundamental points in the Daishonin's teachings and are extremely significant in deepening one's faith. In this work, the term *yuiju ichinin kechimyaku sojo* is introduced, which describes how the Daishonin transmitted and entrusted the Heritage of the Entity of the Law to a single person, the Second High Priest Nikko Shonin, who then transmitted the Buddha's inner enlightenment and entirety of his teachings to the Third High Priest Nichimoku Shonin. It is our hope that this book will help deepen the faith of the Nichiren Shoshu priesthood and laity and help promote the worldwide propagation of the true Law through shakubuku. During the compilation and editing process of this book, we received valuable material from many individuals that enabled us to publish this work. We would like to extend our deepest appreciation to them.

The Study Department of Nichiren Shoshu Head Office
November 2011

Contents

Nichiren Daishonin's Life

The Portrait of our Founder, Nichiren Daishonin, called *Kagami-no-miei*
stored at Head Temple Taisekiji

1. From the Birth to the Establishment of True Buddhism

Viewing the sun rising from Mt. Kiyosumi (Kamogawa City, Chiba Prefecture)

The Buddhism of the sun emerges to illuminate the darkness of the Latter Day of the Law. Nichiren Daishonin chanted the Daimoku of Nam-Myoho-Renge-Kyo to the rising sun, thereby establishing true Buddhism.

The Birth

Nichiren Daishonin was born in Kataumi of Tojo Village in Awa Province (currently Kamogawa City, Chiba Prefecture), on February 16th in the first year of Jo'o (1222). His parents named him Zennichimaro.

It is said that when he was born, clear water sprung from the ground and lotus flowers blossomed on the surface of the ocean near his house.

The scene of Nichiren Daishonin's birth

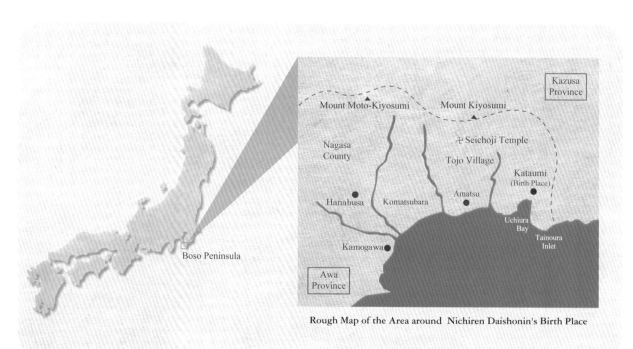

Rough Map of the Area around Nichiren Daishonin's Birth Place

Entering the Priesthood

Zennichimaro enters Seichoji Temple

A giant Japanese cedar tree at Mount Kiyosumi

In the first year of Tempuku (1233), Zennichimaro entered Seichoji Temple near his home. As an acolyte he studied hard, keeping in his heart the pledge, "I also prayed...that I would become the wisest person in Japan."

At the age of 16, he took the tonsure and entered the priesthood, under his master Dozen-bo. He changed his name to Zesho-bo Rencho.

Travel to Various Temples for Study

Rencho sets out on his travels for study

Rencho made a round of visits to various temples of various sects, to places such as Kamakura, which was the political and economic center of Japan in the Kamakura period. He visited Enryakuji Temple at Mount Hi'ei which, at the time, was an important temple for the study of Buddhism. Continuing his travels, he went to numerous other temples, in order to study Buddhist sutras and scriptures.

Years later, in his Gosho, *Reply to Myoho bikuni* (Myoho bikuni-gohenji), he made the following comments:

For more than twenty years, from the time when I was 16 years old, I visited many temples in various provinces including Kamakura, Kyoto, Mount Hi'ei, Onjoji Temple, Mount Koya, and Tennoji Temple, in order to study very hard.

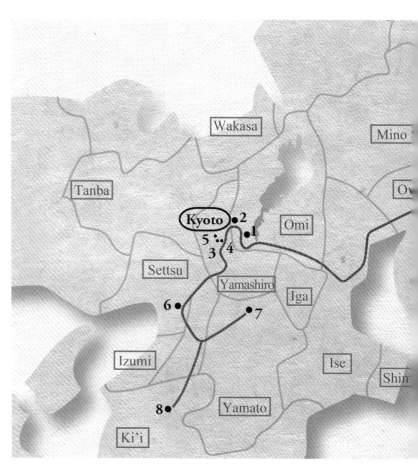

Study at Mount Hi'ei

Trip to Nanto (Yakushiji Temple, Nara City)

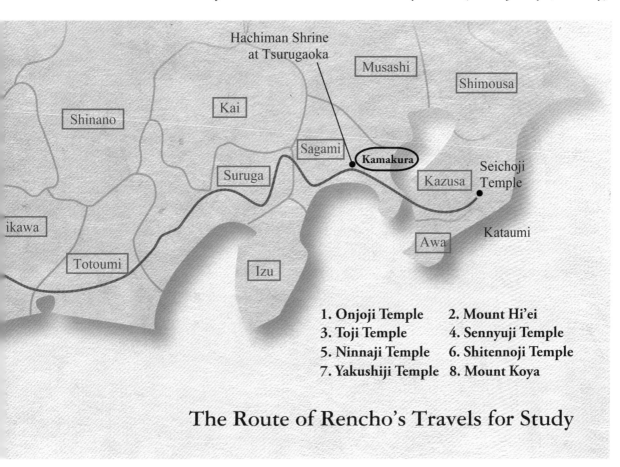

Hachiman Shrine at Tsurugaoka

Musashi

Shimousa

Kai

Shinano

Sagami

Kamakura

Seichoji Temple

Suruga

Kazusa

ikawa

Kataumi

Totoumi

Awa

Izu

1. Onjoji Temple   2. Mount Hi'ei
3. Toji Temple   4. Sennyuji Temple
5. Ninnaji Temple   6. Shitennoji Temple
7. Yakushiji Temple 8. Mount Koya

The Route of Rencho's Travels for Study

The Establishment of True Buddhism

Returning from his travels for study, Rencho climbed to the summit of Kasagamori on Mount Kiyosumi in the early morning of March 28th in the fifth year of Kencho (1253) and chanted the Daimoku of Nam-Myoho-Renge-Kyo to the rising sun. Thus, he declared the establishment of the true Buddhism of sowing of the Latter Day of the Law to the entire universe.

One month later, on April 28th, in the Shobutsubo at Seichoji Temple, Rencho gave a lecture declaring the establishment of true Buddhism. He stated that the Lotus Sutra is the supreme teaching and that all living beings in the Latter Day of the law will be saved only through faith in the teaching Nam-Myoho-Renge-Kyo. He further said that embracing any other teaching would be a huge mistake. At this time, he changed his name to Nichiren.

In his lecture, Nichiren Daishonin warned that upholding the Nembutsu teaching would cause the people to fall into the hell of incessant suffering. Tojo Kagenobu, the lord of Awa province, was a fervent believer of Nembutsu. Listening to the Daishonin's lecture, he became infuriated and tried to attack the Daishonin. However, the Daishonin was able to escape from Seichoji Temple with the help of two senior disciples, Joken-bo and Gijo-bo.

Declaration of the Establishment of True Buddhism at Kasagamori on Mount Kiyosumi

Nichiren Daishonin's first sermon in the Shobutubo at Seichoji Temple *(Shoten porin)*

The Daimoku of Nam-Myoho-Renge-Kyo

Regarding the Daimoku of Nam-Myoho-Renge-Kyo, Nichiren Daishonin states: "Myoho-Renge-Kyo is not simply the text or its meaning. It is the essence of the entire sutra." This passage means that the Daimoku [that Nichiren propagates] is not merely the title of the Lotus Sutra. It is the ultimate truth hidden in the depths of the Life Span of the Tathagata (*Nyorai juryo*; sixteenth) chapter of the essential teaching of the Lotus Sutra.

The Daishonin also teaches: "It is only through the five characters of Myo-Ho-Ren-Ge-Kyo, the seed of enlightenment, that all the Buddhas of the three existences and the ten directions have attained Buddhahood."

In this passage, he reveals that the Daimoku of Nam-Myoho-Renge-Kyo contains the benefits of all the Buddhist teachings.

Therefore, all living beings in the Latter Day of the Law will be able to attain enlightenment, by chanting Nam-Myoho-Renge-Kyo to the Gohonzon.

2. Propagating True Buddhism in Kamakura

The Nagoe Kiridoshi Path (Kamakura City, Kanagawa Prefecture)

Having established the true Law, Nichiren Daishonin went to Kamakura, which was the political and economical center of Japan at the time, in order to carry out the salvation of the people by the Lotus Sutra. He built a small, thatched hut at Matsubagayatsu, Nagoe. There, he exerted himself in propagating true Buddhism.

The Hut at Matsubagayatsu

Nichiren Daishonin took up residence in the hut he built in Nagoe of Matsubagayatsu, Kamakura. He lived there for 18 years, from August of the fifth year of Kencho (1253) to September of the eighth year of Bunnei (1271). While he was there, he preached the Daimoku of the Lotus Sutra, the true Law, and refuted the errors of other sects.

A priest visiting Nichiren Daishonin's hut and requesting to become his disciple

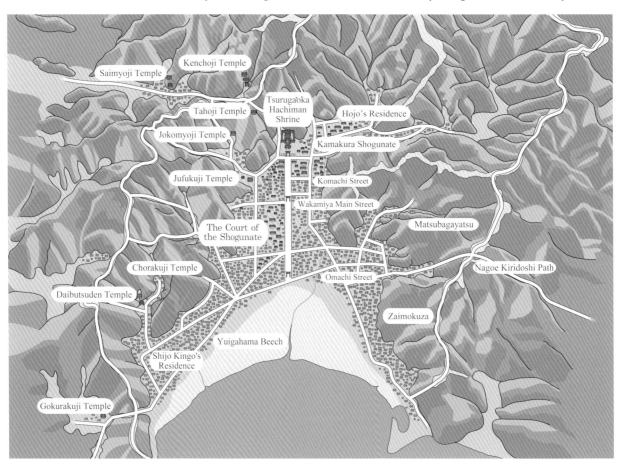

Saimyoji Temple
Kenchoji Temple
Tahoji Temple
Tsurugaoka Hachiman Shrine
Hojo's Residence
Jokomyoji Temple
Kamakura Shogunate
Jufukuji Temple
Komachi Street
Wakamiya Main Street
The Court of the Shogunate
Matsubagayatsu
Chorakuji Temple
Omachi Street
Nagoe Kiridoshi Path
Daibutsuden Temple
Zaimokuza
Yuigahama Beech
Shijo Kingo's Residence
Gokurakuji Temple

A panoramic view of Kamakura in the 13th century

Preaching on the Streets *(Tsuji seppo)*

Nichiren Daishonin began refuting the heresy of the other sects and revealing the truth. He did this while preaching to the public on the streets of Kamakura. He denounced erroneous teachings stating, "Nembutsu leads to the hell of incessant suffering," "Zen is the teaching of devils," and so on. Some people who heard these words spoke ill of Nichiren Daishonin. They persecuted him in various ways, such as cursing him with abusive language, striking him with sticks, and throwing stones at him. Many others, however, were moved by his words and had strong confidence in him. Among them were Shijo Kingo and Toki Jonin, and many other priests and Kamakura samurai warriors.

Nichiren Daishonin preached the true Law; even though he encountered persecution.

The Four Dictums (denouncing the teachings of the four sects)

The Four Dictums are: Nembutsu leads to the hell of incessant suffering; Zen is the teaching of devils; Shingon will ruin the nation; and Ritsu is traitorous. These are the words that Nichiren Daishonin used to refute these four heretical sects in a simple fashion. He also used this language in *Letter to Kenchoji Doryu* (Kenchoji doryu eno onjo), one of the 11 letters that were sent to 11 high-ranking political and religious leaders.

Great Kamakura Earthquakes

In Kamakura, the people were suffering deeply due to constantly occurring natural disasters, such as major earthquakes and epidemics. An especially severe earthquake occurred on August 23rd in the first year of Shoka (1257). It destroyed many shrines and temples in Kamakura and even caused landslides. Many houses collapsed, and fissures in the ground appeared everywhere. Nichiren Daishonin wanted to clarify the cause of these disasters. The following year, he went to the Sutra Storehouse at Jissoji Temple in Iwamoto, Suruga Province (currently Fuji City, Shizuoka Prefecture) and researched the complete collection of the Buddhist scriptures. Finally he wrote the *Rissho ankoku-ron* for the sake of saving all living beings.

A picture of one of the great Kamakura earthquakes

The Sutra Storehouse at Jissoji Temple storing
the complete collection of the Buddhist scriputres

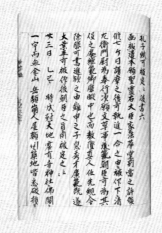

Hojo Edition of the *Azuma-kagami*
(Property of the National Archives of Japan, Cabinet Library)
It states on August 23rd in first year of Shoka (1257) "There are no shrines or temples, not even one building."

A Chronology of Disasters in Kamakura from 1257 to 1260

- August 1, 1257 (first year of Shoka): A great earthquake

- August 23, 1257: Another great earthquake, known as the Great Earthquake of Shoka

- November 8, 1257: Another great earthquake

- November 22, 1257: A major fire

- January 17, 1258 (second year of Shoka): A major fire

- June 24, 1258: Heavy winds and an unseasonable cold spell with winter level temperatures

- August 1, 1258: Torrential rains and wind, which damaged many farms in the area

- October 16, 1258: Torrential rains and flooding in Kamakura

- Spring, 1259 (first year of Shogen): A great famine and a major epidemic

- April 29, 1260 (first year of Bunno): A major fire

- June 1, 1260: Heavy winds and floods in Kamakura

The Submission of the *Rissho ankoku-ron*

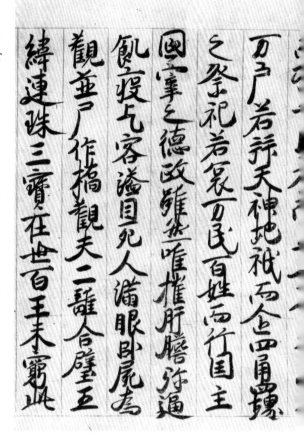

You must immediately renounce your erroneous belief and take faith in the supreme teaching of the one vehicle of the Lotus Sutra.

(*Rissho ankoku-ron*)

Nichiren Daishonin wrote the *Rissho ankoku-ron* as a document of remonstration against the sovereign of the nation. He wrote this treatise for the sake of the salvation of all mankind and the realization of the Buddha land. On July 16th of the first year of Bunno (1260), he submitted it to Hojo Tokiyori, who was the highest authority at that time, through Yadoya nyudo. This is known as the first remonstration with the government.

The *Rissho ankoku-ron* is presented to Hojo Tokiyori

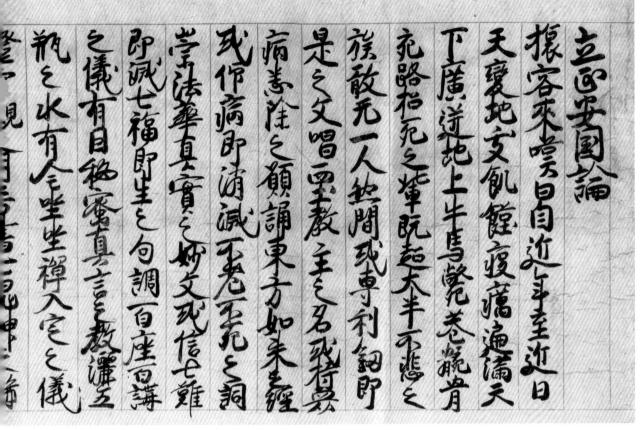

An original copy of the *Rissho ankoku-ron* in Nichiren Daishonin's own calligraphy
stored at Nakayama Hokekyoji Temple

Rissho ankoku-ron

The title, *Rissho ankoku-ron*, means to establish the true teaching and secure the peace of the land. This text is written in the form of questions and answers between a host and his guest, and results in the guest converting to the true Law in the end. In the text, Nichiren Daishonin teaches that all people had gone against the correct Law and had become completely devoted to evil doctrines. This caused all the guardian deities to abandon the country. Furthermore, evil demons had rushed in to take their place, in order to create disasters. The Daishonin predicted that if the people did not stop making offerings to heretical religions and instead take faith in the correct Law of the Lotus Sutra, then two of the seven disasters listed in the sutras that had not yet happened definitely would occur. These disasters were invasion from foreign lands and revolt within one's domain. Therefore, he urged the people, through remonstrating with the sovereign, to immediately renounce their erroneous beliefs and take faith in true Buddhism.

3. Putting the Teaching of the Lotus Sutra into Practice

After remonstrating with Hojo Tokiyori, by submitting the *Rissho ankoku-ron*, Nichiren Daishonin was persecuted by monks and believers of other sects, and also by the government authorities. This persecution was predicted in the twenty-line verse of the Encouraging Devotion (*Kanji*; thirteenth) chapter of the Lotus Sutra, which states: "In the evil age, there will be ignorant people who will speak ill of the practitioner who propagates the true Law. They will curse him, and assault him with swords and staves."

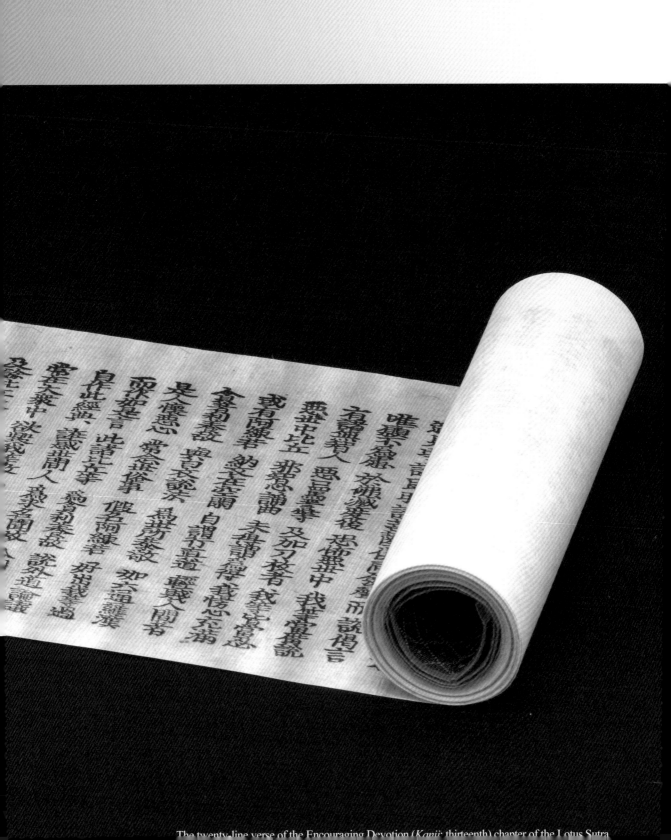

The twenty-line verse of the Encouraging Devotion (*Kanji*; thirteenth) chapter of the Lotus Sutra

The Matsubagayatsu Persecution

The disciples defending Nichiren Daishonin in the persecution

After the submission of the *Rissho ankoku-ron*, influential priests of the Zen, Nembutsu, and Ritsu sects conspired with Hojo Shigetoki in a plot to kill Nichiren Daishonin.

A large group of believers, mainly from the Nembutsu sect, attacked Nichiren Daishonin's hut in Matsubagayatsu. Nichiren Daishonin was able to escape, due to the protection given to him by his disciples and believers.

Matsubagayatsu area (Kamakura City, Kanagawa Prefecture)

The Izu Exile

Disciples and believers sending Nichiren Daishonin off to Izu Peninsula, where he would live in exile

On May 12th in the first year of Kocho (1261), after escaping the attack at Matsubagayatsu, Nichiren Daishonin was exiled to Kawana, Ito, in Izu Peninsula. Regarding the significance of this persecution, Nichiren Daishonin said in the *Four Debts of Gratitude* (Shi'on-sho) that he was "reading the Lotus Sutra with his body" and living "according to the Buddha's words." Funamori Yasaburo, his wife, and other believers took care of the Daishonin while he was living in exile in Izu.

Nichiren Daishonin arriving at his place of exile

The Komatsubara Persecution

Tojo Kagenobu's attack against Nichiren Daishonin

In the autumn of first year of Bunnei (1264), Nichiren Daishonin returned to his family home in Awa Province, in order to pray for the recovery of his mother, who was ill. On October 11th of the same year, the Daishonin was assaulted by a group of Nembutsu believers, lead by Tojo Kagenobu, the lord of Awa Province. He was attacked at the main road of Matsubara, on his way to the residence of Kudo Yoshitaka, the lord of Amatsu province.

During this attack, his disciples Kyonin-bo and Kudo Yoshitaka lost their lives. Nichiren Daishonin suffered a wound on his forehead from a sword, and his left arm was broken.

The Komatsubara area (Kamogawa City, Chiba Prefecture)

A Mongolian Envoy Arrives and Eleven Letters of Remonstration

In the beginning of fifth year of Bunnei (1268), an envoy from the Mongolian empire arrived in Japan and presented a letter to the Kamakura Government demanding that Japan become a vassal state. Thus, the prediction of "invasion from foreign lands" came true.

Nichiren Daishonin sent 11 letters to the persons in power in the Kamakura government including the regent Hojo Tokimune and to seven major temples in Kamakura, asking for a public debate. None of the recipients responded.

The 11 letters of remonstration were sent to the following recipients:

1 Hojo Tokimune
2 Yadoya sa'emon Mitsunori
3 Hei-no sa'emon-noj-o Yoritsuna
4 Hojo Yagenta
5 Doryu, the Head of Kenchoji Temple
6 Ryokan, the Head of Gokurakuji Temple
7 The Head of Daibutsuden Temple
8 Jufukuji Temple
9 Jokomyoji Temple
10 Tahoji Temple
11 Chorakuji Temple

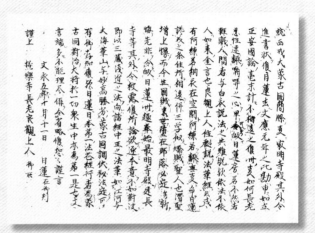

Transcribed copy of
Letter to Ryokan of Gokurakuji Temple

The ship carrying a Mongolian envoy

4. The Tatsunokuchi Persecution

Nichiren Daishonin revealed his true identity as the True Buddha of the infinite past of *kuon-ganjo* by discarding his provisional identity as Bodhisattva Jogyo at the time of the Tatsunokuchi Persecution.

The view when looking toward Enoshima Island from the vicinity of the Tatsunokuchi execution site
(Fujisawa City, Kanagawa Prefecture)

Remonstration against Hei-no sa'emon-no-jo Yoritsuna

On September 10th in the eighth year of Bunnei (1271), due to the slander spread by Ryokan, the chief priest of Gokurakuji Temple, Nichiren Daishonin was summoned to undergo questioning by the chief constable, Hei-no sa'emon-no-jo Yoritsuna. Two days later, on September 12th, the Daishonin sent Yoritsuna a letter. This Gosho is called *On the Day before Yesterday* (Issaku jitsu-gosho). In it, he remonstrated a second time to [immediately discard erroneous teachings and] uphold and practice the Lotus Sutra. On the evening of the same day, Yoritsuna sent hundreds of warriors to close in on the Daishonin's hut in Matsubagayatsu, where they ransacked his residence and proceeded to arrest him. During this time, one of Yoshitsuna's warriors, Sho-bo took a scroll of the fifth volume of the Lotus Sutra from inside the Daishonin's robe and struck him with it three times on the head. Ironically, the fifth volume contains the Encouraging Devotion (*Kanji*; thirteenth) chapter, which states that when propagating the Lotus Sutra in the Latter Day of the Law, one will meet with great persecutions with swords and staves. The Daishonin then turned toward Yoritsuna and scolded him, saying "Nichiren is the master of Japan; killing Nichiren means toppling the pillar of Japan." (*The Selection of the Time* [Senji-sho]) This is known as the second remonstration with the government.

Sho-bo struck Nichiren Daishonin with the fifth volume of the Lotus Sutra

On Route toward the Tatsunokuchi Execution Site

Tonight I will be beheaded...

On the Buddha's Behavior (Shuju onfurumai-gosho)

On September 12th in the eighth year of Bunnei (1271), Nichiren Daishonin was arrested and taken from his thatched dwelling in Matsubayagatsu and dragged around Kamakura City as though he were a serious criminal. He then was brought to the court for sentencing. He was charged with treason and given an official sentence by Hei-no sa'emon-no-jo Yoritsuna to be exiled to Sado Island. However, this was a sentence in appearance only. The government's true intention was to execute the Daishonin, and a plot had been contrived towards this end. Thus, in the middle of the night, the Daishonin was taken to the execution grounds at Tatsunokuchi Beach to be beheaded. On route to Tatsunokuchi, upon passing Tsuruga'oka Hachiman Shrine, the Daishonin dismounted his horse. He reprimanded Bodhisattva Hachiman, insisting he protect the Votary of the Lotus Sutra as the Bodhisattva had promised. Later on, as they passed Yuigahama and approached Goryo Shrine, the Daishonin dispatched a boy named Kumao-maru to inform Shijo Kingo of what was happening. Shijo Kingo immediately came to the Daishonin's side and accompanied him, vowing to take his own life [if the Daishonin were beheaded].

Nichiren Daishonin reprimanding Bodhisattva Hachiman

The Road Traveled on Route to the Execution Site

September 12th in the eighth year of Bunnei (1271) in the middle of the night

1. Leaving the court after sentencing
   [Kamakura (Wakamiya) Shogunate]
2. Reprimanding Bodhisattva Hachiman
3. Yuigahama Beach
4. In front of Goryo Shrine
5. Koshigoe
6. Arriving at the Tatsunokuchi execution site

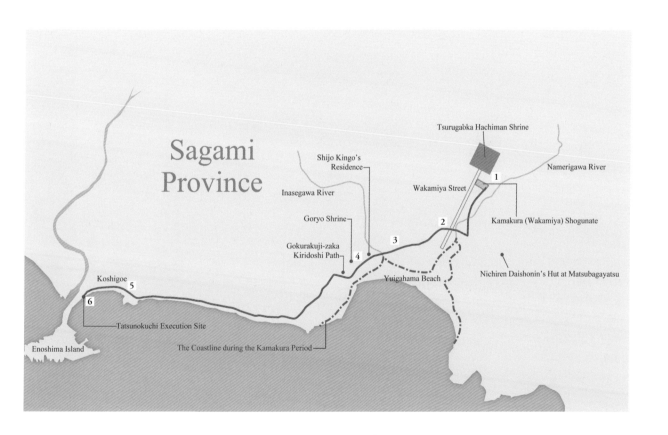

Nichiren Daishonin, upon arriving at the Tatsunokuchi execution site, seated himself upright in the spot where he was to be beheaded. At the moment when the executioner raised his sword over the Daishonin's head, a glowing moon-like orb suddenly appeared in the sky to the southwest of Enoshima Island. The glaring brightness of the orb blinded the executioner, causing him to collapse while the warriors scrambled in fear. Some fell to the ground and prostrated themselves before the Daishonin. In the end, the attempt to behead the Daishonin was unsuccessful.

Discarding the Provisional Identity and Revealing the True Identity (*hosshaku kempon*)

The Tatsunokuchi Persecution is deeply significant in that Nichiren Daishonin discarded his transient identity as Bodhisattva Jogyo (provisional identity, *suijaku-shin*) up until then to reveal his true identity as the True Buddha of *kuon-ganjo* (true identity, *honchi-shin*). This is called *hosshaku kempon*. In regards to this, Nichiren Daishonin states in *The Opening of the Eyes* (Kaimoku-sho): "A man by the name of Nichiren was beheaded [as a common mortal] between the hours of the Rat and Ox on the 12th of the September in the previous year. His soul has reached Sado Island..." (*Gosho*, p. 563) The "soul" that the Daishonin refers to in this passage indicates his soul as the True Buddha of *kuon-ganjo*. Through undergoing the Tatsunokuchi Persecution, which almost cost him his life, the Daishonin revealed his life condition as the True Buddha of *kuon-ganjo*.

The view looking toward Enoshima Island from Tatsunokuchi Shichirigahama
(Fujisawa City, Kanagawa Prefecture)

Homma Residence in Echi

The guardian deity of the stars descending upon the branches of a plum tree

After the failed execution attempt at Tatsunokuchi, Nichiren Daishonin was moved to the residence of Homma Rokuro sa'emon in Echi, Sagami Province (currently Atsugi City, Kanagawa Prefecture). On the evening of September 13th, when the Daishonin stepped out into the large garden of the Homma residence, he turned toward the moon and admonished it. Then, a luminous object suddenly fell from the sky and hung suspended before him in the branches of a plum tree. In *Reply to Shijo Kingo* (Shijo kingo dono-goshosoku), the Daishonin referred to the phenomena, such as the bright orb appearing at the execution site and this luminous object falling before him: "As of yet, two of the three heavenly gods have protected me. Gatten, the guardian deity of the moon, appeared as a bright orb at Tatsunokuchi and saved my life. Four or five days ago, Myojoten, the guardian deity of the stars greeted me." (*Gosho*, p. 479). He made this statement to illustrate that this was proof by the guardian deities (*shoten zenjin*) that they would serve to protect the Daishonin.

5. The Sado Exile

The significance of the Sado Exile within Nichiren Daishonin's teachings is that on Sado, he began to reveal the true teachings and the Gohonzon from the standpoint of his true identity as the True Buddha of *kuon-ganjo*, namely, the votary of the Lotus Sutra in the Latter Day of the Law.

Viewing Sado Island from Teradomari beach (Nagaoka City, Ni'igata Prefecture)

To Sado Island

After being detained at the Homma residence in Echi for almost one month, Nichiren Daishonin departed on October 10th in the eighth year of Bunnei (1271) to begin the trip to Sado Island. After passing Teradomari in Echigo Province (currently Nagaoka City, Ni'igata Prefecture) on the 28th of the same month, he arrived at Matsugasaki in Sado Province (currently Sado City, Ni'igata Prefecture). There, he was instructed to live in the Sammaido at Tsukahara. The Daishonin was transferred to Ichinosawa during the summer of the following year (the ninth year of Bunnei, 1272). During his approximate two and a half year exile, Abutsu-bo and his wife Sennichi ama, Ko nyudo and his wife, Nakaoki nyudo, and Sairen-bo took faith in the teachings of Nichiren Daishonin.

Sado Island

Nichiren Daishonin as he crosses the rough seas to Sado Island

The road traveled to and from Sado

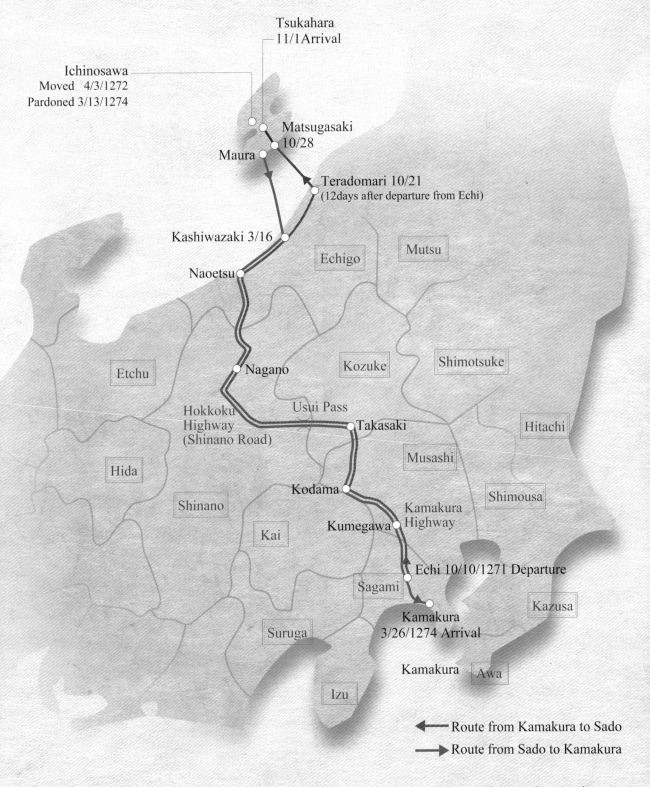

Tsukahara
11/1 Arrival

Ichinosawa
Moved   4/3/1272
Pardoned 3/13/1274

Matsugasaki
10/28

Maura

Teradomari 10/21
(12days after departure from Echi)

Kashiwazaki 3/16

Echigo

Mutsu

Naoetsu

Nagano

Kozuke

Shimotsuke

Etchu

Usui Pass

Hokkoku
Highway
(Shinano Road)

Takasaki

Hitachi

Musashi

Hida

Kodama

Shimousa

Shinano

Kumegawa

Kamakura
Highway

Kai

Echi 10/10/1271 Departure

Sagami

Kazusa

Kamakura
3/26/1274 Arrival

Suruga

Kamakura

Awa

Izu

⟵ Route from Kamakura to Sado

⟶ Route from Sado to Kamakura

The Sammaido at Tsukahara

The Sammaido at Tsukahara was located behind the temporary residence of the deputy constable of Sado Island, Homma Rokuro sa'emon Shigetsura. It was a six foot square hut, and was located in a place where corpses were abandoned. Not even a single statue of the Buddha was anywhere in sight. The Daishonin describes the conditions at the Sammaido in *On the Buddha's Behavior* (Shuju onfurumai-gosho): "the roof and walls were full of holes. The snow fell and piled up, never melting away. I spent night and day there on a fur mat, wearing a straw cape. At night, it constantly hailed and snowed with thunder and lightning. Even in the daytime, the sun hardly shone. (*Gosho*, p. 1062)

Abutsu-bo watching Nichiren Daishonin, before following him

The Tsukahara Debate

Nichiren Daishonin debating hundreds of priests from various sects

Starting on January 16th in the ninth year of Bunnei (1272), over a period of two days, Nichiren Daishonin, at the request of Homma Shigetsura, deputy constable of Sado Island, debated with several hundred priests of various sects. They were completely defeated. When the debate ended, the Daishonin, predicting that a battle soon would break out in Kamakura, urged Homma to quickly return there with his men. One month later, in February, this prediction came true. Hojo Tokisuke, an elder half-brother of the Regent Hojo Tokimune, made an unsuccessful attempt to seize power. Due to this prediction coming true, Homma developed deep respect for the Daishonin. This led him to become a believer.

Homma Shigetsura converting and becoming Nichiren Daishonin's follower

The Opening of the Eyes (Kaimoku-sho) and The True Object of Worship (Kanjin no honzon-sho)

During the Sado exile, the Daishonin wrote over 50 Goshos. Among these Goshos, *The Opening of the Eyes* and *The True Object of Worship* represent two of his most important lifetime works.

The Opening of the Eyes was written in February of the ninth year of Bunnei (1272) at the Sammaido in Tsukahara. This major writing reveals that the Daishonin himself is the Votary of the Lotus Sutra in the Latter Day of the Law. He declares that he is the True Buddha, who possesses the three virtues of sovereign, teacher and parent. This writing reveals the object of worship in terms of the person.

The Opening of the Eyes (Kaimoku-sho)
transcribed copy

Kuninaka plain and Tsukahara impression (Meguro Town, Sado City)

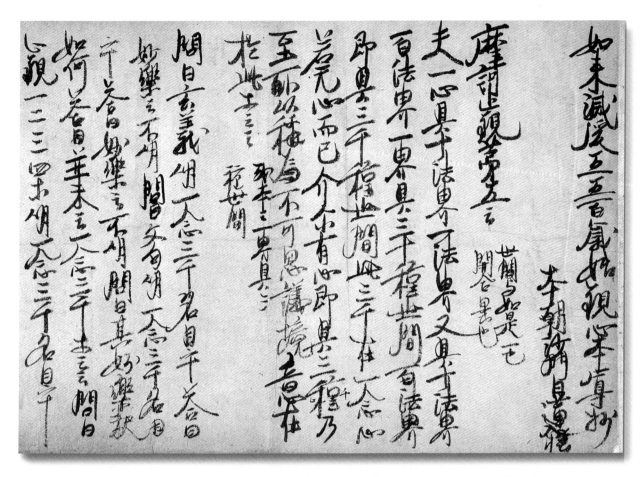

An original manuscript of *The True Object of Worship* in Nichiren Daishonin's own calligraphy stored at Nakayama Hokekyoji Temple

The True Object of Worship was written at Ichinosawa and dated April 25th in the tenth year of Bunnei (1273). This work reveals the object of worship in terms of the Law *(ho-honzon kaiken no sho)*. In this Gosho, the Daishonin reveals that the True Buddha makes his advent in the beginning of the Latter Day of the Law and identifies the true object of worship hidden in the depths of the *Juryo* chapter of the Lotus Sutra. This is the object of worship that will lead all living beings to Buddhahood.

Ichinosawa surrounding area (Ichinosawa, Sado City)

Pardon

Witnessing the flight of a white headed crow, said to be a good omen preceding a pardon

In February of the 11th year of Bunnei (1274), Nichiren Daishonin climbed a mountain nearby and strongly admonished the guardian deities. The Daishonin's determination and life force shook the entire realm of the ultimate reality. He then saw a white headed crow fly by. Historically, this was said to be a good omen preceding a pardon.

The regent Hojo Tokimune issued a pardon to the Daishonin on the 14th of February. On March eighth, the notice of pardon arrived on Sado Island.

Five days later, on March 13th, the Daishonin left Ichinosawa and reached a harbor called Maura, from where he set sail on the next day. He arrived in Kamakura on the 26th of that same month.

Nichiren Daishonin's Deep Gratitude to the Sado Believers

The Daishonin's exile came to an end after two years and five months. He spent this time under extremely harsh conditions in Sado. Finally, he was able to return to Kamakura.

During the time of his exile, his supporters, such as Abutsu-bo, his wife Sennichi-ama, Ko nyudo, and his wife Ko ama, protected him in secrecy. Referring to them, he wrote the following in *Letter to Ko ama* (Ko ama gozen-gosho): "My life in Sado was harsh, indeed, but I truly was reticent to leave. Each time I took a step, something seemed to be pulling me back. I felt as if my heart always would remain there." (*Gosho*, p. 740)

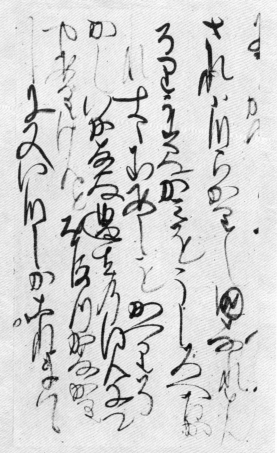

An original manuscript of Nichiren Daishonin's Gosho *Letter to Ko ama*, stored at Nakayama Hokekyoji Temple

Maura Harbor, where Nichiren Daishonin departed for his trip back to Kamakura (currently Maura, Sado City)

6. Entering Mount Minobu and Training his Disciples

After his pardon from the Sado Exile, Nichiren Daishonin returned to Kamakura and remonstrated with the government for the third time. His admonitions, however, were ignored, and this led Nichiren Daishonin to make the decision to leave Kamakura and live in retirement.

He departed Kamakura and went to Mount Minobu, where he took up residence, focusing on writing his teachings, and training his disciples.

Mount Fuji seen from Minobu (currently Minobu Town, Yamanashi Prefecture)

Nichiren Daishonin remonstrating with Yoritsuna

The Third Remonstration with the Government

After returning to Kamakura, Nichiren Daishonin met with government officials, including Hei-no sa'emon-no-jo Yoritsuna, on April 8th in the 11th year of Bunnei (1274). This is called the third remonstration with the Government. The Daishonin replied to Yoritsuna's questions, explaining that none of the other religious teachings can lead the people to attain enlightenment. He declared that the Mongols would invade Japan that same year. He remonstrated with the officials, urging them to uphold the true teaching immediately. However, Yoritsuna did not heed the Daishonin's words.

The Three-time Distinction

The three-time distinction indicates the three remonstrations Nichiren Daishonin conducted with the government. *The Selection of the Time* (Senji-sho) states: "I have now gained the three-time distinction."

The first remonstration was on July 16th, the first year of Bunno (1260), when he submitted the *Rissho ankoku-ron* to the highest authority in the nation, Hojo Tokiyori.

The second remonstration was on September 12th, the eighth year of Bunnei (1271), when the Daishonin remonstrated with Hei-no sa'emon-no-jo Yoritsuna, after he had attacked Nichiren Daishonin's hut and arrested him.

The third remonstration was on April 8th, 1274, when the Daishonin remonstrated again with Hei-no sa'emon-no-jo Yoritsuna after being pardoned from the Sado Exile.

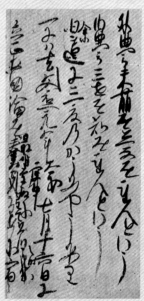

An original manuscript of *The Selection of the Time*, in Nichiren Daishonin's own calligraphy, stored at Tamazawa Myohokkeji Temple

Entering Mount Minobu

Following the maixm, "If one's remonstrations are refused three times, one should leave and retire in the mountains," Nichiren Daishonin decided to retire with honor. Following Nikko Shonin's recommendation, Nichiren Daishonin left Kamakura on May 12th in the 11th year of Bunnei (1274), and went to Mount Minobu in Kai Province (Minobu Town, Yamanashi Prefecture) where he would live in retirement. Hakiri Sanenaga, the lord of Minobu, was a believer who had been converted to the Daishonin's Buddhism by Nikko Shonin.

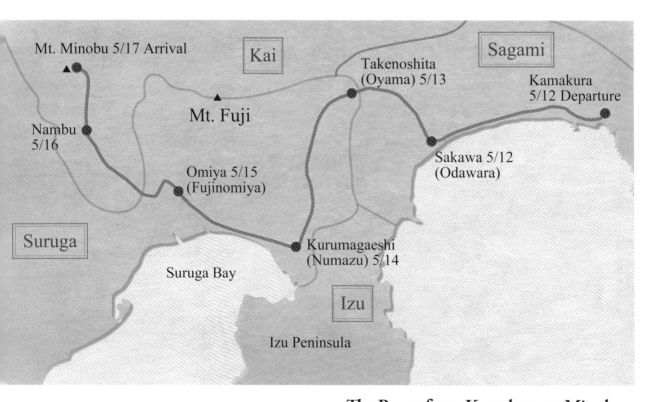

The Route from Kamakura to Minobu

The hut in Minobu

Residence in Minobu

Nichiren Daishonin's hut was built in a narrow valley, surrounded on all four sides by Mount Tenshigatake, Mount Shichimen, Mount Takatori, and Mount Minobu. The valley also was surrounded by four rivers: the Fujikawa, Hayakawa, Hakiikawa, and Minobukawa.

Nichiren Daishonin states in *On the Buddha's Behavior* (Shuju onfurumai-gosho):

"There is no sun to be seen in the daytime, and no moon at night. In winter there is deep snow, and in summer the grass grows thick. There are no tracks to follow, because people seldom come to see me."

The spot that is recognized as
the location of the hut
(Minobu Town, Yamanashi Prefecture)

Life in Minobu

It was cold in winter. The Daishonin was ill-nourished and ill-clad. He stated in *On Offering of an Unlined Cloth* (Hitoeginu-sho): "I eat snow to prolong my life, and wear straw cloaks to ward off the cold. When there are no nuts to harvest, I go hungry for two or three days. When my moccasins fall apart, I have no shoes to wear for three or four months."

The Daishonin lived quite humbly. He did receive Gokuyo offerings from believers, but it was not enough to take care of the many disciples living there with him.

Nanjo Tokimitsu transporting offerings to Nichiren Daishonin in Mount Minobu as Gokuyo

Training Disciples

Sounds of the recitation of the Lotus Sutra Resonating in the sky
Words of debate on the One Vehicle teaching Reverberating in the mountain

On the Forgotten Sutra Book (Boji kyo ji)

Nichiren Daishonin devoted himself to train his disciples at Minobu. He gave lectures on the profound doctrines of the Lotus Sutra and many other important principles.

Nichiren Daishonin wrote detailed descriptions of the situation in Minobu. In *Reply to Soya* (Soya dono-gohenji), he stated: "This year, there are 100 people to nourish in the mountains. They are studying and reciting the Lotus Sutra all night and all day."

There are more than 500 writings of Nichiren Daishonin that exist today. More than 300 of them were written during the nine-year period of the Daishonin's residency in Minobu.

Nichiren Daishonin giving a lecture to his disciples

7. The Atsuwara Persecution and the Establishment of the Dai-Gohonzon of the High Sanctuary of the Essential Teaching

Atsuwara and the surrounding region (Fuji City, Shizuoka Prefecture)

Prompted by the sincere peasant believers who upheld the spirit of not begrudging one's life for the sake of the Law *(fujishaku shinmyo)* during the Atsuwara persecution, Nichiren Daishonin inscribed the Dai-Gohonzon of the High Sanctuary of the Essential Teaching, the ultimate purpose of his advent into this world.

Nikko Shonin's Propagation Efforts in the Fuji Region

When Nichiren Daishonin took up residence at Minobu, Nikko Shonin served the Daishonin and also exerted himself to propagate the true Law in the Suruga and Fuji regions. Because of his efforts, a number of priests of Ryusenji Temple in Atsuwara and many peasant farmers took faith in the Daishonin's teaching.

Nikko Shonin propagated Nichiren Daishonin's teaching in the Fuji region

The Atsuwara Persecution

The Atsuwara believers under attack

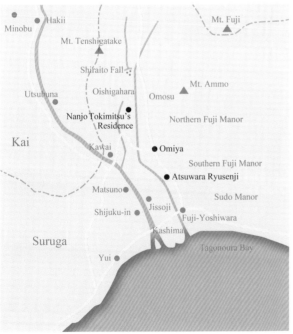

A simple map of the locations related to
the Atsuwara Persecution

Opposed to Nikko Shonin's propagation efforts
in Fuji, Gyochi, the deputy chief priest of
Ryusenji Temple, plotted to persecute Nichiren
Daishonin's lay believers in Atsuwara province.
In the second year of Ko'an (1279), Gyochi's
oppression became even more severe. He
arrested 20 peasant believers and sent them to
Kamakura, falsely accusing them of illegally
harvesting rice.

The Atsuwara Believers under pressure to discard their faith

The Three Atsuwara Martyrs

As soon as he received an urgent message reporting the conditions of the Atsuwara persecution, Nichiren Daishonin wrote a petition to the High Court of Kamakura, which is called *The Ryusenji Petition* (Ryusenji moshijo), and waited for news on the proceedings in the Kamakura Court. Hei-no sa'emon-no-jo Yoritsuna and his son Iinuma hangan tortured the Atsuwara believers. They shot them with toad-eye arrows (meant to inflict pain rather than cause fatal injury). They threatened the believers and demanded that they discard their faith in the Daishonin's teachings. The Atsuwara believers, however, never submitted and continued chanting the Daimoku. Yoritsuna lost his temper, and ordered the three leaders of the peasant believers, Jinshiro, Yagoro, and Yarokuro, to be beheaded.

The Toad-eye Arrow

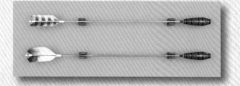

This arrow had a wooden head in the shape of a turnip with holes drilled into it. The name, *hikime*, originates from the appearance of the turnip-shaped arrowhead, which looked like the eyes of a toad. These arrows, which made a whistling sound as they flew, were said to exorcise demons.

Fourteen years after the Atsuwara persecution occurred, Hei-no sa'emon-no-jo Yoritsuna was executed on charges of rebellion. It can be said that this was a manifestation of punishment for slandering the Lotus Sutra.

The Monument of the Three Atsuwara Martyrs
(located on the grounds of Head Temple Taisekiji)

Having established the Dai-Gohonzon, Nichiren Daishonin fulfilled the ultimate purpose of his advent.

The Ultimate Purpose of Nichiren Daishonin's Advent into this World:
Establishment of the Dai-Gohonzon of The High Sanctuary of the Essential Teaching

Nichiren Daishonin observed the sincerity of the peasant believers in Atsuwara, who never begrudged their lives. On October 12th in the second year of Ko'an (1279), Nichiren Daishonin inscribed the Great Mandala of Nam-Myoho-Renge-Kyo on a huge, thick camphor wood plank. He instructed his disciple, Izumi-ko Nippo, to be in charge of carving his inscription. Thus, the Daishonin established the Dai-Gohonzon, the ultimate purpose of his advent.

This Gohonzon is the supreme object of worship, which manifests the oneness of the person and the Law. In the Gosho, *Reply to Kyo'o* (Kyo'o dono-gohenji), The Daishonin states, "I, Nichiren, with sumi, have infused my life [into the Gohonzon]. So believe in it." (*Gosho*, p. 685)

This Gohonzon will be enshrined in the High Sanctuary of Hommonji Temple at the time of kosen-rufu. Therefore, it is called the Dai-Gohonzon of the High Sanctuary of the Essential Teaching.

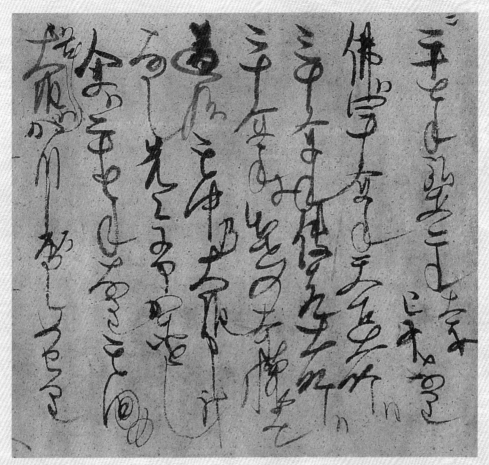

An original manuscript of *On Persecutions Befalling the Buddha* in Nichiren Daishonin's own calligraphy stored at Nakayama Hokekyoji Temple

The Ultimate Purpose of One's Advent

The ultimate purpose of one's advent *(shusse no hongai)* refers to the true purpose of the Buddhas' and bodhisattvas' advent into this world.

Regarding the ultimate purpose of his advent into this world, Nichiren Daishonin made the following declaration in *On Persecutions Befalling the Buddha* (Shonin gonan ji), "It has taken me twenty-seven years." (*Gosho*, p. 1396) He stated that he fulfilled his ultimate purpose around the time of the 27th anniversary of his declaration of the establishment of true Buddhism in the fifth year of Kencho (1253).

8. The Transmission of the Heritage of the Law and the Demise of Nichiren Daishonin

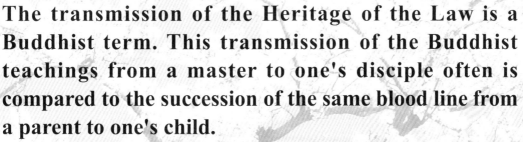

The transmission of the Heritage of the Law is a Buddhist term. This transmission of the Buddhist teachings from a master to one's disciple often is compared to the succession of the same blood line from a parent to one's child.

From his many disciples, Nichiren Daishonin selected Nikko Shonin as the one and only successor, and transmitted the entirety of true Buddhism to him. Then on October 13th in the fifth year of Ko'an (1282), Nichiren Daishonin peacefully entered nirvana.

Mount Fuji and the cherry blossoms in all of their glory at Head Temple Taisekiji

Transmitting the Law at Mount Minobu

The Transmission at Mount Minobu

In September of the fifth year of Ko'an (1282), Nichiren Daishonin bestowed *Document for Entrusting the Law that Nichiren Propagated throughout his Life* (Nichiren ichigo guho fuzokusho) to Nikko Shonin, as proof of the transmission of the Heritage of the Law, entrusted to a single person.

In this writing, the Daishonin designated Nikko Shonin as the Great Master of Propagation of the Essential Teaching. He was to be the leader of all the priesthood and laity. The Daishonin further instructed that at the time of kosen-rufu, the High Sanctuary of Hommonji Temple must be established.

The Daishonin was in poor health, and his disciples urged him to go to the hot springs to recuperate. On September 8th in the same year, the Daishonin left Minobu to visit the hot springs in Hitachi Province. He was escorted by Nikko Shonin and other disciples. He arrived at the residence of Ikegami Munenaka in Musashi Province (currently Ota Ward, Tokyo).

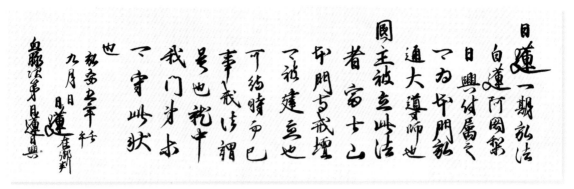

Transcribed copy of *Document for Entrusting the Law that Nichiren Propagated throughout his Life*

Document for Entrusting the Law that Nichiren Propagated throughout his Life (Nichiren ichigo guho fuzokusho)

I, Nichiren, transfer the entirety of the Law that I have propagated throughout my life to Byakuren Ajari Nikko, and designate him the Great Master of Propagation of the Essential Teaching. When the sovereign embraces this Law, establish the [True] High Sanctuary of Hommonji Temple at Mount Fuji. You must await the time. This is the actual precept of the Law.

Above all else, my disciples must obey this document.

The ninth month in the fifth year of Ko'an (1282)

Nichiren (signature mark)

The order of the Heritage of the Law: from Nichiren to Nikko

Nichiren Daishonin departing from Mount Minobu escorted by his disciples

Transmitting the Law at Ikegami

The Transmission at Ikegami

On October eighth in the fifth year of Ko'an (1282), Nichiren Daishonin selected six senior priests. Furthermore, on the thirteenth day of the same month, he appointed Nikko Shonin as the chief priest of Minobu-san Kuonji Temple. This was recorded in the *Minobu-san Transfer Document* (Minobu-san fuzokusho).

In this document, the Daishonin strictly admonished the priests and lay believers that those who disobeyed Nikko Shonin, who inherited the Heritage of the Law, would be going against Nichiren Daishonin's Buddhism and commit slander of the true Law.

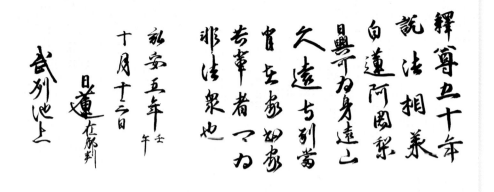

Minobu-san Transfer Document (**Minobusan fuzokusho**)

I transfer Shakyamuni Buddha's teachings of fifty years to Byakuren Ajari Nikko. He is to be the chief priest of Minobu-san Kuonji Temple. Laity or priests who disobey him go against the Law.

The thirteenth day of the tenth month in the fifth year of Ko'an (1282)

Ikegami, Bushu Province

Nichiren (signature mark)

A lecture on the *Rissho ankoku-ron*

Nichiren Daishonin giving lecture on the *Rissho ankoku-ron*

On September 18th the fifth year of Ko'an (1282), Nichiren Daishonin arrived at the residence of Ikegami Munenaka in Musashi Province. There, he gave a lecture to his disciples and lay believers on the principles of the *Rissho ankoku-ron*. This lecture signifies the Daishonin's admonishment that all the believers should advance toward the achievement of kosen-rufu with the spirit of "One's life is insignificant, while the Law is supreme. You should be willing to give your life to propagate the Law." Because of this last lecture, it has been said since olden times that "Nichiren Daishonin's life begins and ends with the *Rissho ankoku-ron*."

Nichiren Daishonin peacefully passing away surrounded by his disciples and lay believers

The Demise of Nichiren Daishonin

On October 13th in the fifth year of Ko'an (1282), at the hour of the Dragon (approximately 8:00 AM), Nichiren Daishonin tranquilily passed away at the age of 61.

It is said that at that time, the ground suddenly trembled, and the cherry blossoms in the garden bloomed all at once, even though it was the begining of winter.

The demise of the Daishonin does not merely signify his entry into nirvana. It is the manifestation of the mystic aspect of non-extinction within extinction. It signifies that the True Buddha Nichiren Daishonin's eternal life remains as the Dai-Gohonzon of the High Sanctuary of the Essential Teaching. Thus, he eternally saves all living beings.

The entire funeral ceremony for Nichiren Daishonin was held under the direction of Nikko Shonin, who had been designated by the Daishonin as the Great Master who inherited the Heritage of the Law.

After the funeral, Nikko Shonin officiated the memorial ceremony on the seventh day following the Daishonin's passing. In the early morning of October 21st, he left Ikegami with the ashes of Nichiren Daishonin and returned to Mount Minobu on 25th of the same month.

Funeral procession of Nichiren Daishonin

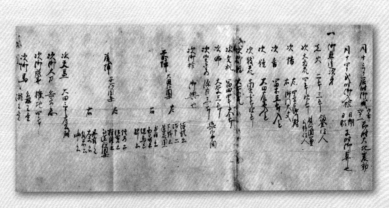

Record of the Passing of our Founder (Shuso gosenge kiroku)

Written by Nikko Shonin, stored at Nishiyama Hommonji Temple

This writing was left by Nikko Shonin as the document chronicling Nichiren Daishonin's funeral ceremony.

It also records the Daishonin's legacy, his selection of the six major disciples just before his passing, and his instructions on how to handle both the statue of Shakyamuni Buddha and the copy of the Lotus Sutra that Nichiren Daishonin possessed while he was alive.

Abbreviated Chronological Table of the Life of Nichiren Daishonin

Before the Declaration of the Establishment of True Buddhism

Year	Date	Age	Occurence
1222 (the first year of Jo'o)	2.16	1	Born in Kataumi located in Tojo Village of Awa Province. His given name at birth was Zennichimaro.
1233 (the first year of Tenpuku)	Spring	12	Entered Seichoji Temple in Awa Province.
1237 (the third year of Katei)		16	Formally entered the priesthood under Dozen-bo. His name was changed to Zesho-bo Rencho.
1241 (the second year of Ninji)		20	Read the entire Buddhist scriptures at Tsurugaoka Hachiman Shrine in Kamakura.
1242 (the third year of Ninji)		21	Made the journey to Mount Hiei for study.
1246 (the fourth year of Kangen)		25	Made the journey to Onjoji Temple and the temples in Nara for study. Visited Sennyuji Temple in Kyoto.
1247 (the first year of Hoji)		26	Read the complete collection of the Buddhist scriptures at Yakushiji Temple.
1248 (the second year of Hoji)		27	Made the journey to Mount Koya, Onjoji Temple and other temples for study. He then went to Toji Temple and Nin'naji Temple in Kyoto for further study.
1249 (the first year of Kencho)		28	Returned to Mt. Hi'ei and stayed in Joko-in Temple.
1250 (the second year of Kencho)		29	Made the journey to Shiten'noji Temple in Settsu Province for study.
1252 (the forth year of Kencho)	August	31	Left Mt. Hi'ei and made the journey to Onjoji Temple for study.
1253 (the fifth year of Kencho)	3.28	32	Privately made the inner declaration of the establishment of True Buddhism at Seichoji Temple
	4.28		Preached the True Buddhism at Seichoji Temple and declared the establishment of True Buddhism.
			Renamed himself Nichiren and conducted the Gojukai ceremony for his parents.

Period in Kamakura

Year	Date	Age	Occurence
			Began propagating in Kamakura, living in a hut at Matsubagayatsu.
1257 (the first year of Shoka)	8.23	36	A great earthquake completely destroyed all the temples and shrines in Kamakura.
1258 (the second year of Shoka)		37	Read the complete collection of the Buddhist scriptures at Jissoji Temple in Iwamoto of Suruga Province.
			Allowed Kai-ko (Nikko Shonin) to be his disciple and named him Hoki-bo.

Year	Date	Age	Occurence
1258 (the second year of Shoka)	2.14	37	The Daishonin's father Nukina Jiro Shigetada (Myonichi) passed away.
1260 (the first year of Bunno)	7.16	39	Submitted the *Rissho ankoku-ron* to Hojo Tokiyori. [First Remonstration with the Government]
	8.27		Assaulted at his hut in Matsubagayatsu. [Matsubagayatsu Persecution]
1261 (the first year of Kocho)	5.12	40	Exiled to Kawana in Ito of Izu Province. Nikko Shonin accompanied him. [Izu Exile]
1263 (the third year of Kocho)	2.22	42	Returned to Kamakura after being pardoned from exile.
1264 (the first year of Bunnei)	11.11	43	Assaulted by Lord Tojo Kagenobu and his vassals at Komatsubara in Tojo Village of Awa Province. [Komatsubara Persecution]
1267 (the forth year of Bunnei)	8.15	46	The Daishonin's mother Umegiku (Myoren) passed away.
1268 (the fifth year of Bunnei)	Intercalary 1.18	47	A letter from the Mongol empire was delivered to the Kamakura government demanding Japan become a vassal state.
	10.11		Wrote and sent letters of remonstration to 11 recipients, known as *The Eleven Letters of Remonstration* (Juittsu gosho).
1271 (the eighth year of Bunnei)	July	50	Ryokan and others made false accusations against the Daishonin to those in power in the Kamakura government.
	9.10		Summoned to the High Court and personally interrogated by Hei-no sa'emon-no-jo Yoritsuna.
	9.12		Sent a letter to Hei-no sa'emon-no-jo Yoritsuna urging him to reflect on the behavior he demonstrated toward the Daishonin and his true Buddhism.
			Arrested in his hut at Matsubagayatsu.
			Remonstrated with Hei-no sa'emon-no-jo Yoritsuna. [Second Remonstration with the Government]
			Transported late at night under escort to the execution grounds at Tatsunokuchi.
			On the way to the execution grounds, he stopped at Tsurugaoka Hachiman Shrine and admonished the Great Bodhisattva Hachiman.
			Between the hours of the Rat and the Ox (Approximately 12:00 AM to 2:00 AM), he escaped being beheaded at Tatsunokuchi by the mystic appearance of a luminous object. [Tatsunokuchi Persecution]

Year	Date	Age	Occurence
1271 (the eighth year of Bunnei)	9.13	50	Transferred to the residence of Lord Homma in Echi of Sagami Province.
			Arrived at the residence of Lord Homma in Echi approximately at noon.
			At night, the mystic appearance of a bright star occurred.

Period in Sado Island

Year	Date	Age	Occurence
1271 (the eighth year of Bunnei)	10.10		Left the residence of Lord Homma for Sado Island. Nikko Shonin accompanied him. [Sado Exile]
	10.28		Arrived at Sado Island.
	11.1		Sent to a hut called the Sammaido at Tsukahara. The Daishonin was forced to dwell there.
1272 (the ninth year of Bunnei)	1.16-17	51	Debated with priests of various Buddhist sects at Tsukahara. [Tsukahara Debate]
			Predicted the occurrence of "a revolt from within" to Lord Homma Shigetsura, the deputy of the constable of Sado Province.
	February		Wrote *The Opening of the Eyes* (Kaimoku-sho).
	Summer		Moved to Ichinosawa on Sado.
1273 (the tenth year of Bunnei)	4.25	52	Wrote *The True Object of Worship* (Kanjin no honzon-sho).
1274 (the eleventh year of Bunnei)	2.14	53	The Kamakura government issued a pardon to the Daishonin from the Sado Exile.
	3.8		The pardon arrived at Sado.
	3.13		Left Ichinosawa, accompanied by Nikko Shonin.
	3.26		Arrived in Kamakura.
	4.8		Had a meeting with Hei-no sa'emon-no-jo Yoritsuna and remonstrated with him. [Third Remonstration with the Government]

Period in Mount Minobu

Year	Date	Age	Occurence
1274 (the eleventh year of Bunnei)	5.12	53	Left Kamakura. On the seventeenth day of the same month, arrived at Hakii County in Kai Province.
	6.17		The construction of the Daishonin's hut in Minobusawa was completed.
	10.5		The Mongols invaded Japan. [Battle of Bunnei]
1275 (the first year of Kenji)	6.10	54	Wrote *The Selection of the Time* (Senji-sho).

Year	Date	Age	Occurence
1276 (the second year of Kenji)	7.21	55	Wrote *Repaying Debts of Gratitude* (Ho'on-sho).
1278 (the first year of Ko'an)	1.1	57	Completed the *Orally Transmitted Teachings on the Lotus Sutra* (Ongi kuden), approving the manuscript of his lecture that was transcribed by Nikko Shonin.
	3.19		Began a lecture on the Lotus Sutra for his disciples. [*Recorded Lectures* (Onko kikigaki)]
1279 (the second year of Ko'an)	9.21	58	20 lay believers of Atsuwara in Fuji of Suruga Province were arrested and taken to Kamakura on false charges.
	10.12		Inscribed the Dai-Gohonzon of the High Sanctuary of the Essential Teaching. [Ultimate Purpose of Nichiren Daishonin's Advent]
	10.15		Three lay believers of Atsuwara, Jinshiro, Yagoro, and Yarokuro were beheaded.
1281 (the fourth year of Ko'an)	5.21	60	The Mongols invaded Japan again. [Battle of Ko'an]
1282 (the fifth year of Ko'an)	4.8	61	Wrote *On the Transmission of the Three Great Secret Laws* (Sandai hiho bonjo ji).
	September		Bestowed the *Document for Entrusting the Law that Nichiren Propagated throughout his Life* (Nichiren ichigo guho fuzokusho) to Nikko Shonin and designated him as the Great Master of Propagation of the Essential Teaching.
	9.8		Left Mt. Minobu for the hot-springs in Hitachi Province.
	9.18		Arrived at Ikegami of Musashi Province.
	9.25		Lectured on the *Rissho ankoku-ron* for his disciples and lay believers.
	10.8		Selected six senior disciples.
	10.13		Bestowed the *Minobusan Transfer Document* (Minobusan fuzokusho) upon Nikko Shonin and inaugurated him as the Chief Priest of Minobu-san Kuonji Temple.
	10.13		At the hour of the Dragon (approximately 8:00 AM), Nichiren Daishonin passed away.
	10.14		At the hour of the Dog (approximately 8:00 PM), the Daishonin's body was placed in a coffin. At the hour of the Rat (around midnight), his funeral ceremony was held.
	10.16		Nikko Shonin wrote *Record of the Passing of our Founder* (Shuso gosenge kiroku).
	10.21		Nikko Shonin left Ikegami with the ashes of Nichiren Daishonin.
	10.25		Nikko Shonin returned to Mount Minobu.

The Second High Priest Nikko Shonin and Taisekiji Temple

A Portrait of the Second High Priest Nikko Shonin
stored at Head Temple Taisekiji

The Accomplishments of Nikko Shonin

"You must not in the least deviate from the way our master propagated the doctrines of the Fuji School."

(*Twenty-six Admonitions of Nikko* [Nikko yuikai okimonn])

The Second High Priest Nikko Shonin was born at Kajikazawa in Oi Village in Kai Province (currently Fujikawa Town, Yamanashi Prefecture) on March 8th in the fourth year of Kangen (1246). In the second year of Shoka (1258), he became a disciple of Nichiren Daishonin, and took the name Hoki-bo. (Later, his name was changed to Byakuren Ajari Nikko.)

Nikko Shonin always faithfully and constantly served the Daishonin and strived to propagate the Daisonin's Buddhism in various places.

In the fifth year of Ko'an (1282), he inherited the entirety of Nichiren Daishonin's Buddhism from the Daishonin, and became the chief priest of Minobu-san Kuonji Temple.

Seven years later, however, slander was rampant in Mount Minobu. Hakiri Sanenaga, the feudal lord of Minobu, had repeatedly committed slanderous acts against the true Law. Thus, Nikko Shonin left Mount Minobu in order to protect the purity of the Daishonin's true Buddhism. He founded Taisekiji Temple in the Fuji-Ueno region (currently Fujinomiya City, Shizuoka Prefecture) in the following year. Thereafter, Nikko Shonin moved to the Omosu area and established a seminary for Buddhist study. There, he concentrated on training his disciples.

In the second year of Genko (1332), Nikko Shonin designated Nichimoku Shonin as the Master of the Seat of the Law of Jambudvipa (the entire world). He peacefully passed away on February 7th in the third year of Genko (1333).

Faithfully and Constantly Serving Nichiren Daishonin and Propagating True Buddhism.

Hoki-bo (Nikko Shonin) entreating Nichiren Daishonin to become his disciple

Nikko Shonin became a disciple of Nichiren Daishonin when the Daishonin visited Jissoji Temple at Iwamoto in Suruga province (currently Fuji City, Shizuoka Prefecture) to peruse the complete collection of the Buddhist scriptures for his research. From then on, Nikko Shonin accompanied the Daishonin, even during the Izu Exile in the first year of Kocho (1261), the Tatsunokuchi Persecution in the eighth year of Bunnei (1271), and the Sado Exile that followed.

While faithfully and constantly serving the Daishonin, Nikko Shonin endeavored to propagate the Daishonin's teachings. His efforts expanded into the areas of Izu, Sado, Kai, and Fuji. Many priests and lay people were converted to the Daishonin's teaching.

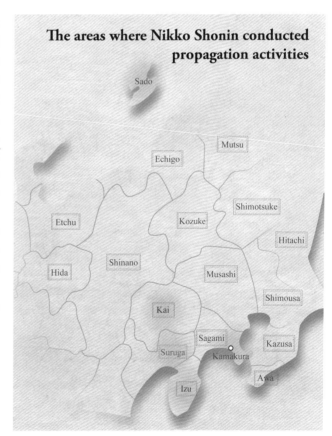

The areas where Nikko Shonin conducted propagation activities

Sado

Mutsu

Echigo

Shimotsuke

Etchu

Kozuke

Hitachi

Shinano

Hida

Musashi

Shimousa

Kai

Sagami

Suruga

Kamakura

Kazusa

Awa

Izu

Becoming the Chief Priest of Kuonji Temple

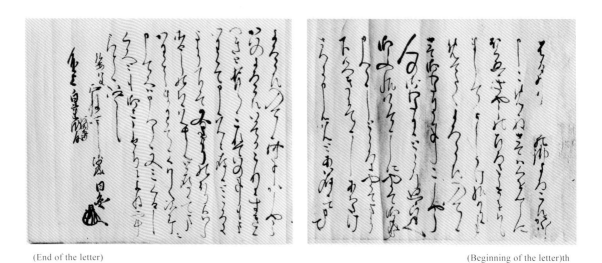

(End of the letter)

(Beginning of the letter)th

The Letter from Hakiri Nichien (Hakiri nichien jo), stored at Nishiyama Hommonji Temple

On October 25th in the fifth year of Ko'an (1282), Nikko Shonin returned to Mount Minobu with the ashes of Nichiren Daishonin. He then assumed his position of the Chief Priest of Minobu-san Kuonji Temple.

The lord of [Kai Province], Hakiri Sanenaga (Nichien) recorded his feelings in a letter he wrote to Nikko Shonin in the eighth year of Ko'an (1285). He stated: "I am extremely pleased that the propagation of the mystic Law *(Myoho)* is spreading throughout the Minobu area by Nikko Shonin. I believe that Nikko Shonin residing at Mount Minobu carries the same significance as Nichiren Daishonin existing there."

A Minobu mountain stream (Minobu Town, Yamanashi Prefecture)

Nikko Shonin leaving Mount Minobu with the sacred treasures

Leaving Mount Minobu

Around the beginning of spring in eighth year of Ko'an (1285), Minbu Niko, one of the major disciples of Nichiren Daishonin, visited Mount Minobu. Nikko Shonin was pleased to see him and appointed Niko as the head teacher of priests at Minobu. However, Niko began to demonstrate inappropriate behavior toward the Law. He asked an artist to paint a Mandala. Niko then manipulated the lord, Hakiri Sanenaga, who committed "four slanderous acts." They were: making a donation to erect a statue of Shakyamuni Buddha, visiting heretical shrines, making a donation to erect a Nembutsu tower, and building a heretical temple—Kuhon Nembutsu Temple. Nichiren Daishonin had stated that if the lord of the region committed slander of the Law, he would not reside there. Following the Daishonin's will, Nikko Shonin decided to leave Mount Minobu. In the spring of the second year of Sho'o (1289), Nikko Shonin left Mount Minobu with all of the sacred treasures, including the Dai-Gohonzon of the High Sanctuary of the Essential Teaching. He then stayed for awhile at the home of his maternal grandfather of Kawai-nyudo. Soon after, he was invited to stay in the home of the lord of Fuji-Ueno, Nanjo Tokimitsu, who was a strong believer from the time Nichiren Daishonin was still alive. Nikko Shonin's departure from Mount Minobu and arrival in Fuji-Ueno was caused by Hakiri Sanenaga's slandering of the Law. His true intention, however, was to carry out Nichiren Daishonin's great will—"establish the [True] High Sanctuary of Hommonji Temple at Mount Fuji."

Nikko Shonin and Nanjo Tokimitsu await
the completion of the edifice

The Establishment of Taisekiji Temple

Having moved to Fuji-Ueno, Nikko Shonin accepted
a donation of land in the area of Oishi-ga-hara from
the lord Nanjo Tokimitsu. On October 12th in the
third year of Sho'o (1290), he established Taisekiji
Temple, creating the foundation for the eternal
propagation of true Buddhism. Before the temple
opened, Nikko Shonin preached to his disciples
standing on top of a large stone on the property.

Nikko Shonin's preaching stone on the grounds of
Taisekiji (2.2 meters high) that is called *Seppo-ishi*

Nanjo Tokimitsu, the Founding Lord of Taisekiji

Nanjo Tokimitsu was the son of Nanjo Hyoe Shichiro. He was born in the first year of Shogen (1259). His father passed away when he was only seven years old, so Tokimitsu devoted himself to practice with his mother. As a young lord, he frequently visited Nichiren Daishonin in Mount Minobu and brought offerings, even when he and his familiy were suffering from want. During the Atsuwara Persecution, Tokimitsu dedicated himself to lead the members in the Fuji region, harboring the believers who were being persecuted. Due to his devotion during the Atsuwara Persecution, the Daishonin granted him the title of "Lord Ueno, the Wise." After the demise of Nichiren Daishonin, when Nikko Shonin departed Mount Minobu, Tokimitsu invited him to stay at his estate. Moreover, he offered a tract of land called Oishi-ga-hara to Nikko Shonin and exerted himself toward the establishment of Taisekiji. In his later years, Tokimitsu became a lay priest called Daigyo. He passed away at the age of 74 on May first in the second year of Genko (1332).

The Image Hall *(Mieido)* at Head Temple Taisekiji

The Perpetuation of the Law

Nikko Shonin put his heart and soul into training his disciples for many years. In the second yeaer of Genko (1332), he wrote *Articles to be Observed after the Passing of Nikko* (Nikko ato jojo no koto). It states:

> • The Dai-Gohonzon of the second year of Ko'an (1279), which Nikko inherited [from Nichiren Daishonin], is hereby bequeathed to Nichimoku. It should be enshrined at Hommonji Temple.

> • Taisekiji, including the main hall and the cemetery, should be administered by Nichimoku, who also should maintain the premises, conduct Gongyo and await the time of kosen-rufu.

As it reads, Nikko Shonin transferred both the Dai-Gohonzon of the High Sanctuary of the Essential Teaching and Taisekiji which is the fundamental place of faith and practice for kosen-rufu to Nichimoku Shonin.

On January of the next year, Nikko Shonin complied the principles and formalities of Nichiren Shoshu into 26 articles called *The Twenty-six Admonitions of Nikko* (Nikko yuikai okimon). This is his guidance to the Nichiren Shoshu believers for the future, lasting ten-thousand years and more. Thus, Nikko Shonin made great efforts for the perpetuation of the Law, in order to ensure the eternal transmission of the true teaching to future generations.

Abbreviated Chronological Table of the Life of Nikko Shonin

Year	Date	Age	Occurence
1246 (the fourth year of Kagen)	3.8	1	Born in Kajikazawa, located in Oi Village of Kai Province.
1258 (the second year of Shoka)		13	Entered the priesthood as Nichiren Daishonin's disciple. The Daishonin named him Hoki-bo.
1261 (the first year of Kocho)	5.12	16	Accompanied the Daishonin to the Izu Exile.
1271 (the eighth year of Bunnei)	10.10	26	Accompanied the Daishonin to the Sado Exile.
1282 (the fifth year of Ko'an)	September	37	*Document for Entrusting the Law that Nichiren Propagated throughout his Life* (Nichiren ichigo guho fuzokusho) was bestowed on him by the Daishonin.
	10.13		*Minobu-san Transfer Document* (Minobusan fuzokusho) was bestowed on him by the Daishonin. At the hour of the Dragon (approximately 8:00 AM), Nichiren Daishonin passed away.
	10.16		Wrote *Record of the Passing of our Founder* (Shuso gosenge kiroku).
	10.21		Left Ikegami with the ashes of the Daishonin. On the twenty-fifth day of the same month, Nikko Shonin arrived at Mt. Minobu.
1285 (the eighth year of Ko'an)		40	When Niko made a pilgrimage to Mt. Minobu, Nikko Shonin appointed him as the head teacher of priests.
1289 (the second year of Sho'o)		44	Due to the slanderous actions of Hakiri Sanenaga (Nichien), Nikko Shonin left Mt. Minobu and stayed at the residence of the Nanjo family at Fuji-Ueno.
1290 (the third year of Sho'o)	10.12	45	Established Taisekiji Temple.
	10.13		Privately transmitted the Heritage of the Law, entrusted to a single person to Nichimoku Shonin and bestowed the Gohonzon of the Seat of the Law (*Joza* Gohonzon) upon him.
1298 (the sixth year of Einin)	2.15	52	Built an Image Hall at Omosu and moved there.
1332 (the second year of Genko) [the first year of Shokyo]	10.10	87	Bestowed *Articles to be Observed after the Passing of Nikko* (Nikko ato jojo no koto) upon Nichimoku Shonin and designated him as the Master of the Seat of the Law for the entire world.
1333 (the third year of Genko)	1.13	88	Set forth the *Twenty-six Admonitions of Nikko* (Nikko yuikai okimon).
	2.7		Passed away at Omosu.

The Third High Priest Nichimoku Shonin and his Aspiration for Kosen-rufu

A Portrait of the Third High Priest, Nichimoku Shonin
Stored at Head Temple Taisekiji

The Legacy of Nichimoku Shonin

"Generations shall pass, And our determination shall amass
At the foot of Mount Fuji, Like smoke that reaches far beyond the clouds."
(Nichimoku Shonin's deathbed poem)

The Third High Priest, Nichimoku Shonin, was born in the first year of Bunno (1260) in Hatake Village in Ni'ida County of Izu Province (currently Hatake, Kannami Town, Tagata County, Shizuoka Prefecture). His birth name was Toraomaru. His mother was a sister of Nanjo Tokimitsu. While Nikko Shonin was propagating Nichiren Daishonin's Buddhism in Izu, Nichimoku Shonin became his disciple. Afterwards, he went to Mount Minobu and constantly served Nichiren Daishonin. He received the name Kunaikyo-no-kimi, and later was given the name Ni'ida-Kyo Ajari.

Nichimoku Shonin traveled the provinces of the Tohoku and Tokai regions in order to propagate the Daishonin's Buddhism. Furthermore, he remonstrated with the Kamakura government and the Imperial Court 42 times during his lifetime.

On October 13th in the third year of Sho'o (1290), Nichimoku Shonin privately received the transmission of the Heritage of the Law from Nikko Shonin. On November 10th in the second year of Genko (1332), Nikko Shonin transferred the Dai-Gohonzon of the High Sanctuary of the Essential Teaching to Nichimoku Shonin, and designated him as the Master of the Seat of the Law. In October of the following year (1333), Nichimoku Shonin transfered the Heritage of the Law to the Fourth High Priest Nichido Shonin. In the same year, on November 15th, Nichimoku Shonin passed away in Tarui, Mino province, on the way to Kyoto, to remonstrate with the imperial court.

Continuous and Faithful Service to his Master

Nichimoku Shonin began to serve his true master, Nichiren Daishonin, at the age of 17, after he became Nikko Shonin's disciple. While devoting himself to study, Nichimoku Shonin served the Daishonin at Mount Minobu for seven years, until the Daishonin's demise in the fifth year of Ko'an (1282).

Several times every day, in order to serve the Daishonin, Nichimoku Shonin walked down to mountain streams in Minobu to draw fresh water. There is a legend stating that because he often carried a pail of water on top of his scalp, he developed a flat spot on his head.

There is a poem that reads, "I grasped the Lotus Sutra through serving my master—by cutting firewood, gathering greens, and drawing water." This poem clearly demonstrates how Nichimoku Shonin dedicated himself to serve his master.

Nichimoku Shonin's constant dedication in serving Nichiren Daishonin

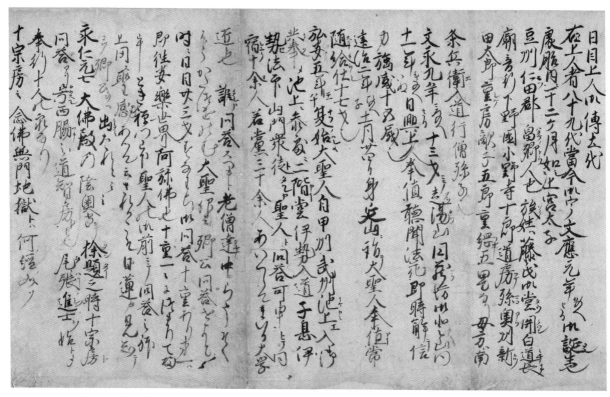

A Biography of the Masters (Godendodai) written by the Fourth High Priest Nichido Shonin stored at Head Temple Taisekiji

The Great Debater

In September of the fifth year of Ko'an (1282), when he was 23 years old, following Nichiren Daishonin's directive, Nichimoku Shonin conducted a ten-round debate with a priest of the Tendai sect named Ise-Hoin, the son of Nikaido Ise-no-kami, a Kamakura government official. Nichimoku Shonin won each round of the debate.

The Daishonin was delighted with Nichimoku Shonin's winning in the debate. As a gift for his accomplishment, the Daishonin gave Nichimoku Shonin one of his tooth. This tooth is called the *Goshokotsu*.

In June of the first year of Shoan (1299), Nichimoku Shonin fulfilled a long-held wish, having an opportunity to hold an official debate at Rokuhara in Kyoto. In this debate, Nichimoku Shonin thoroughly defeated Jisshu-bo Dochi, a priest of the Nembutsu teaching. Hojo Munenobu, who later became the eleventh regent of the Kamakura government, had deeply believed in him. This story is described in the writing, *A Biography of the Masters*, which is a biography of the Daishonin, Nikko Shonin, and Nichimoku Shonin.

It has been said that the Daishonin once declared, "Since I entrust Nikko to write and Nichimoku to conduct debates, I have all the disciples that I need."

Remonstration

Nichimoku Shonin conducted a total of 42 remonstrations against the imperial authorities in Kyoto and various samurai clans in Kamakura.

Nikko Shonin bestowed on him a special Gohonzon, praising Nichimoku Shonin's remarkable achievement in remonstrations. On the side of this Gohonzon, Nikko Shonin made the following inscription:

The person who is foremost in remonstration.
The lead disciple among primary disciples, Ni'ida-Kyo Ajari Nichimoku.

In the third year of Genko (1333), the Kamakura Shogunate collapsed, and imperial rule was restored. Nichimoku Shonin set out on a journey to Kyoto, despite his advanced age, to conduct one final remonstration. He passed away, however, on the way to Kyoto, at Tarui in Mino province.

Nichimoku Shonin traveling to Kyoto with his disciples

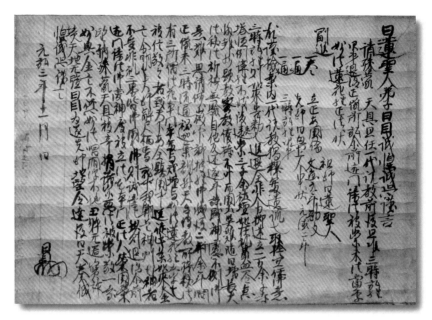

The Last Petition of Nichimoku Shonin, stored at Hota Myohonji Temple

Aspiration for Kosen-rufu

Nichimoku Shonin's deathbed poem reads as follows:

Generations shall pass   **And our determination shall amass**
At the foot of Mount Fuji,   **Like smoke that reaches far beyond the clouds.**

From this poem, we are able to feel Nichimoku Shonin's strong aspiration to achieve kosen-rufu. Even if it takes many lifetimes, his determination to remonstrate with the sovereign never will weaken. Like smoke that reaches far beyond the clouds, the teaching of Myoho-Renge-Kyo from the foot of Mount Fuji will reach to the Imperial Court in Kyoto, and the pledge for kosen-rufu will be achieved without fail.

In our denomination, we honorifically designate Nichimoku Shonin as the Master of the Seat of the Law. This is based on Nikko Shonin's writing, *Articles to be Observed after the Passing of Nikko* (Nikko ato jojo no koto) conferred upon Nichimoku Shonin. It contains the following statement:

When Hommonji Temple is established, Ni'ida-Kyo Ajari Nichimoku is to be Master of the Seat of the Law. (*Gosho*, p. 1883)

There are legends that have been handed down. One states that at the time of kosen-rufu, Nichimoku Shonin will make his advent. An another legend says that all of the successive High Priests are Nichimoku Shonin.

Nichimoku Shonin's aspiration for kosen-rufu and his spirit of protecting the true Law have been transmitted to the successive High Priests until today.

Abbreviated Chronological Table of the Life of Nichimoku Shonin

Year	Date	Age	Occurence
1260 (the first year of Bunno)		1	Born in Hatake Village in the Ni'ida County of Izu Province. His birth name was Tora-o-maru.
1276 (the second year of Kenji)	4.8	17	Entered the priesthood at Enzobo Temple at Mt. Soto as a disciple of Nikko Shonin.
	11.24		Entered Mt. Minobu and began to constantly serve Nichiren Daishonin.
1281 (the forth year of Ko'an)		22	Conducted the *Remonstration against Onjoji Temple* (Onjoji Moshijo). This was his first remonstration on behalf of the Daishonin.
1282 (the fifth year of Ko'an)		23	Held a debate with Ise-Hoin following a directive by the Daishonin. Received the Daishnon's tooth called the *Goshokotsu* after winning the debate.
1283 (the sixth year of Ko'an)		24	Propagation activities in the provinces of Izu and Oshu. (He continued his propagation efforts in Oshu Province during the following two years.)
1290 (the third year of Sho'o)	10.13	31	Privately received the transmission of the Heritage of the Law and the Gohonzon of the Seat of the Law (*Joza* Gohonzon) from Nikko Shonin.
			Established the Renzobo, a sub-temple at Taisekiji.
1298 (the sixth year of Einin)		39	Nikko Shonin designated his six senior disciples headed by Nichimoku Shonin.
1299 (the first year of Shoan)	7.1	40	Won a public debate with Jisshu-bo Dochi at the Rokuhara in Kyoto.
1332 (the second year of Genko) [the first year of Shokyo]	11.10	73	Nikko Shonin gave Nichimoku Shonin *Articles to be Observed after the Passing of Nikko* (Nikko ato jojo no koto) and designated him as the Master of the Seat of the Law.
1333 (the third year of Genko)	2.7	74	Nikko Shonin passed away. Nichimoku Shonin was in charge of the funeral ceremony.
	5.22		The fall of the Kamakura Shogunate
	October		Transmitted the Heritage of the Law to Nichido Shonin.
	11.15		Nichimoku Shonin passed away at Tarui in Mino Province, on the way to remonstrate with the emperor.

― 絵と写真で見る ―

英語版　日蓮大聖人のご生涯と正法伝持

令和2年4月1日　発行

編　　　集　日蓮正宗宗務院
製作・発行　（株）大 日 蓮 出 版　　〒418-0116　静岡県富士宮市上条546-1

ISBN 978-4-905522-90-4